Prague

A PICTORIAL GUIDE
TO THE HISTORIC CITY

ARTFOTO

PRAGUE – A PICTORIAL GUIDE TO THE HISTORIC CITY
Project Editor: Jiří Šourek
Photographs: Jiří Šourek
Text: Hana Bílková, František Kadlec, Václav Ledvinka
Layout: Jiří Šourek
Maps: Věra Petrů
Translation: Norah Hronková
Editors: Hana Bílková
          Ivana Šourková, Milada Lexová and Veronika Mandíková
Published by Artfoto Publishers Prague in 1999 as their 45th publication
2nd edition
Repro and Printed by Tiskárny BNB Velké Poříčí

ISBN 80-86085-35-X

CONTENTS

The Prague Old Town towers.

PRAGUE of a hundred spires, magical, golden, a jewel in the heart of Europe - and photogenic Prague. Those are just a few of the descriptions that visitors to Prague, especially foreigners, have given the city whose delightful scenery in the valleys and on the hills on both banks of the river Vltava has for centuries had such a profound effect on most of its visitors. Prague is a city of unique wide-spread views, as well as of picturesque little nooks and corners. It is a city of legends - about the people's King Wenceslas, the magician Žito and the blinded maker of the famous astronomical clock Master Hanuš, about the eccentric Emperor Rudolph and Rabbi Löw, creator of the fabled Golem. Its unusually well-preserved and numerous monuments to the past form the matchless atmosphere and special local colour of the historic metropolis, where the past is intertwined with the present, dreams with reality, beauty with the bizarre. The genius loci of Prague can be felt in its streets today so intensively, that it can scarcely be paralleled in any other European city.

PRAGUE is the biggest and most important town in the Czech Republic. Since the 9th century it has, without interruption, been the capital of the Czech state. It is the biggest industrial, commercial and financial centre of the country, but mainly a historic monument and a cultural, social and political centre of European significance. The heart of Prague is formed by its historic core, which covers an area of 8.1 square kilometres. It extends over the present district of Prague 1, and a great part of Prague 2. It has only about 70 thousand permanent inhabitants, but several times that number come there every day to work, and every year over 7 million tourists pass through its streets.

This historic core of Prague consists of six original medieval town communities - the Old Town, the New Town, the Little Quarter, Hradčany, the Jewish Town (Josefov) and Vyšehrad. In 1971 all this territory was declared a town memorial reservation. According to the state list of cultural memorial buildings there are over two thousand historical buildings on it, that form a unique urbanist and artistic whole. The centre of Prague is one of the biggest town memorial reservations anywhere and represents rare cultural values of European and world importance. In 1992 the Prague memorial reservation was included in the UNESCO list of World Heritage and was thus recognised as part of the cultural possessions of all mankind.

The roots of Prague's importance today lie in its **thousand years of history as the capital city of the Czech state and the seat of its rulers**. It began with the foundation of Prague Castle by Prince Bořivoj I. of the House of the Přemyslides at some time between 880 and 890. In the first half of the 10th century the other Přemyslide fortress, **Vyšehrad**, came into being on the opposite bank of the river Vltava. The so far scattered settlements gradually came to be concentrated below these two new fortresses. The Arab-Jewish merchant Ibrahim ibn Jakub, who visited Bohemia in 965 or 966, noted the existence here of a busy market place and a town built of stone and mortar. The chronicler Cosmas tells around the year 1100 of rich and flourishing settlements below both Prague Castle and Vyšehrad and communities of German, French, Italian, Spanish and Jewish merchants in them. The first exact evidence of a large **marketplace** on the right bank of the Vltava, where the Old Town Square now is, comes from 1100. And just near it a royal customs house (**Týn-Ungelt**) was set up at some time during the 12th century. Near these again there was extensive building activity, leading to a mass of stone farmsteads, houses, churches and monasteries, built in Romanesque style (the remains are still preserved of

the churches of St. **Martin in the Wall** and **St. Wenceslas** in Zderaz, the rotunda of the **Holy Rood**, the rotunda of **St. Longin** on the Pond, the **house of the lords of Kunštát and of Poděbrady** in Chain Street (Řetězová) and others.) All these were linked to the left-bank settlement below the Castle, dominated by the Premonstratensian **Strahov monastery** by the stone Romanesque Judith Bridge.

The process of birth of a typically **medieval town** reached its peak on the right and left banks of the river Vltava in the 13th century. This was when fortifications were built separating after 1230 the **Prague Town** (later the **Old Town of Prague**) from the other varied buildings. In 1257 King Přemysl Ottakar I. (1253-1278) founded the New Town on the left bank of the river (called since the 14th century the Lesser Town or the **Little Quarter**). The construction inside the town fortifications went on in the new architectural and art style - **Gothic**. The tone was given by the buildings of the monasteries of the knightly and beggarly orders. An excellent memorial that has been preserved since the 13th century is the **Convent of the Poor Clares of St. Agnes** in Na Františku, with the church of St. Francis and the Lady Chapel, founded in 1233 and added to soon afterwards by the adjoining Minorite monastery and the church of St. Saviour. Comparably valuable with the area of St. Agnes from the architectural point of view is the double-naved **Old-New synagogue**, built in the second third of the 13th century in the centre of Prague's **Jewish ghetto**. Its prosperity is connected with the issue of privileges for the Jews of Prague by King Přemysl Ottakar II. in 1255. The dominants of the newly-built Gothic town were again a Minorite church, that of **St. James** and the chapter church of **St. Giles**.

The height of prosperity of these twin towns came about during the reign of Emperor and King Charles IV. (1346-1378). This most important of all the Bohemian medieval rulers systematically reformed Prague to be a prestigious royal seat and a magnificent metropolis of the medieval Roman Empire. He founded a **university** in the town (1348) - the first to the north of the Alps, he made grandiose plans for and founded the **New Town of Prague** (1348), his architects - headed by Matthias of Arras and Petr Parléř - built dozens of both temporal and ecclesiastical buildings (the **cathedral of St. Vitus** with its St. Wenceslas chapel, the **Charles Bridge** and the bridge towers, the **Town Hall of the Old Town**, the monastery **Na Slovanech** (Emmaus), the monastery of **St. Charles the Great in Karlov**, the chapter and church of **St. Apollinaris**, the churches of **St. Henry, St. Stephan** and others). Charles's Prague grew into a splendid high Gothic city, one of the largest in the Europe of that day.

The social quarrels that were hidden beneath the exterior prosperity of Charles's Prague led at the beginning of the 15th century to a reform movement, most importantly represented by John Huss (1372-1415). After Huss had been burnt at the stake this grew into a **revolution** and the first European **religious reform** (1419-1434). Hussite Prague resisted the crusades of King Sigismund and became a decisive power factor in the country. The Czech nobleman George of Poděbrady was elected "Hussite king" in the Town Hall of Prague's Old Town (1458). The revival of the town in illusive late Gothic style - the most important architects being Benedikt Ried and Matěj Rejsek of Prostějov - began with the completion of the church of the **Mother of God Before Týn**, the building of the lofty **Powder Tower** and putting a new facade on the south side of the Town Hall of the Old Town (the portal and the big decorative window are still preserved today), with the **horologe**, with the addition of the lower calendarium, statues and other decoration. It came to a summit in Ried's new **fortifications of Prague Castle**, with the towers called Powder (Mihulka), White and **Daliborka**, and above all in his rebuilding of the royal palace with the vast **throne (Vladislav) Hall**. **5**

The privileged position of post-Hussite Prague was shaken by the accession of the Habsburg dynasty to the Bohemian throne in 1526. After the unsuccessful **rising of the Czech Estates in 1547** Kind Ferdinand I. took economic power and political influence from the people of Prague through confiscations and punishments. Yet in spite of this political and ownership disaster, the Prague towns experienced in the second half of the 16th century a revival of economic life, intensive **Renaissance rebuilding** and a great flourishing of culture. The presence of the court of the enterprising and cultural governor Ferdinand of the Tyrol (1548-1565) attracted to Prague merchants, businessmen, bankers and builders from Italy, south-west Germany and the Netherlands, but also noblemen, who began to build their city **palaces** on the burnt land left after the great conflagration of the left river-bank of Prague in 1541 (Lobkovicz-Schwarzenberg, lords of Hradec, Martinický, Smiřický and others). This process culminated when in 1583-1612 Prague Castle became the seat of the art-loving Emperor Rudolph II. His court became a **gathering-place for artists and learned men** from the whole of Europe. Astronomers and mathematicians worked there, Tycho Brahe and Johannes Kepler, the artists Adrien de Vries, Hans van Aachen, Giuseppe Arcimboldo and Bartholomew Spranger, and also the alchemists John Dee and Edward Kelley, and learned Jews such as Rabbi Jehuda Löw, creator of the famous Golem. The imperial art collections (Kunstkamera) became legendary, as did the wealth and busy life of the rapidly growing town below the Castle. After 1600 Rudoph's Prague became a splendid city with 60,000 inhabitants.

After the fateful **defeat** of the second anti-Habsburg rising by the Czech estates at the **Battle of the White Mountain** (8. 11. 1620), the city of Prague was once more afflicted with harsh punishments, plundering, forced recatholization and the mass emigration of non-catholics. The fact that the imperial court and state offices moved to Vienna gradually degraded Prague into a **provincial town**. In spite of this the imperial generalissimo Albrecht of Valdštejn built his residence in the Little Quarter of Prague in 1623-1630, and the building of other **noblemen's palaces** continued, not to speak of **monasteries and churches** of the reviving catholic church. The creative styles of valuable buildings by J. B. Mathey, J. Santini-Aichl, K. Dientzenhofer, K. I. Dientzenhofer, F. M. Kaňka, together with other famous and also nameless stonemasons, stucco workers, sculptors and painters gave the city after the Battle of the White Mountain its own characteristic style - "**Prague baroque**".

A court decree of Emperor Joseph II., dated 12. 2. 1784, united the four so far independent Prague towns - the Old Town, the New Town, the Little Quarter and Hradčany - into a single **capital city of Prague**. The industrial revolution led to the origin of **industrial suburbs** (Karlín, Smíchov, Holešovice, Libeň) and the enlarged Prague again became a centre of cultural life and of the Czech **national liberation movement**. In 1787 Mozart's opera Don Giovanni had its world premiere in the Nostic (Estates) Theatre in the Old Town, for a number of years C. M. von Weber worked here as a conductor, Beethoven repeatedly gave concerts here, as did other representatives of classicism and romanticism in music.

In June 1848 the Bohemian capital city joined the trend of bourgeois revolutions, and not even the following years of Bach's absolutism (1849-1859) could prevent its becoming a **modern capitalist city**. The Czech bourgeoisie, which dominated the city administration in the first general elections after the fall of absolutism in 1861,

modernized Prague on the model of west European capitals. The large and prestigious buildings of the **National Theatre**, the **National Museum**, the **Rudophinum**, the **Municipal House**, the **New Town Hall** and others were erected. As well as Czech culture and science a typical German-Jewish culture also developed in Prague, represented by such writers as F. Kafka, R. M. Rilke, F. Werfel, G. Meyrink, E. E. Kisch and others. For a longer or shorter time G. Mahler, E. Mach, A. Einstein and others worked here. But a negative result of the modernization was the insensitive **urban renewal of the inner city**. The culutural loss thus incurred was only partly compensated for by the new public and dwelling houses in the styles of Czech neo-Renaissance, Art Nouveau and cubism.

On 28th October 1918 Prague became the **capital city of the independent Czechoslovak Republic**. Its construction introduced a number of new urbanist, architectural and cultural values, carried out in the spirits of **modernism, functionalism and avant-garde artistic trends** of the nineteen-twenties and thirties. The high standard of Prague's interwar architecture is witnessed by such giant buildings as the **Adria Palace**, the **Law faculty**, the **Mánes** building, the **Trade Fair Palace**, the **General Insurance Institute**, the **Electricity Firm**, buildings of various ministries on the Vltava embankments, and others.

Prague maintained its **democratic self-government** until 15. 3. 1939, when it was **occupied** by the army of Nazi Germany. The antifascist resistance of the people of Prague reached its peak with the **Prague May Uprising** from 5th - 9th May 1945, which ended with the liberation of the town, but also meant the destruction of the eastern neo-Gothic wing of the Town Hall of the Old Town.

The forty years of rule by the Czechoslovak Communist Party in Prague (1948-1989) was marked by the tragic crimes of the Stalinist system, and also by lack of qualifications in the city administration. All the same some important urbanist constructions were built (three lines of the underground railway, the Nusle and Barrandov bridges, the department stores Kotva, Družba-Krone, Máj-Tesco and others). Some success was attained in the **renovation of historic buildings** (the overall reconstruction of Prague Castle, the renovation of the convents of St. George and St. Agnes for the National Gallery, the general reconstruction of the National Theatre, renewal of the exteriors along the Royal Route).

Only the "**velvet**" **revolution** of November 1989 put a final end to the totalitarian regime and a revival of the democratic system. The resulting extensive social and economic changes have greatly enlivened the face of the city, especially the historic parts of it, which have again found their dynamism.

Prague on the threshold of the third millennium A. D. is a city that is both historical and contemporary, it is a unique reservation of ancient monuments, but at the same time a lively city organism. It is one of the important political and economic European centres, but especially a cultural one. Its undoubted significance and attraction both for those who live there and for visitors from all corners of the world consists just in the harmony and strange synthesis of the historical traditions of a thousand years, still intensely present in the city's atmosphere, and the dynamic, varied and fascinating life of the present, streaming through the Prague streets.

Václav Ledvinka

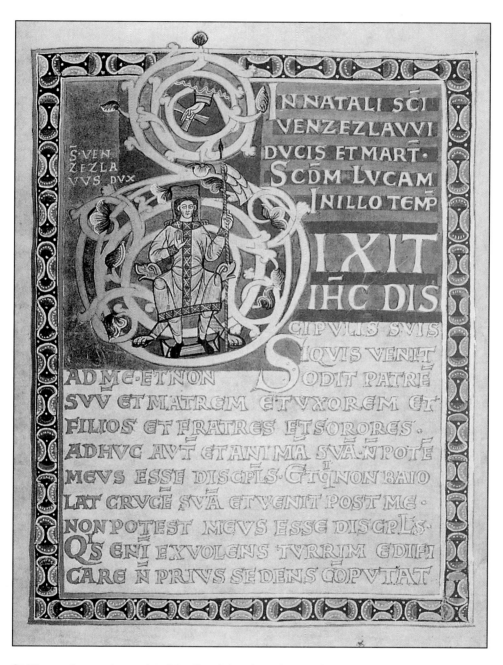

St. Wenceslas - patron saint of the Czech Lands, a drawing from the Vyšehrad Codex, ordered in 1084 for the coronation of the first King of Bohemia, Vratislav II.

PRAGUE – HISTORICAL AREAS MAP

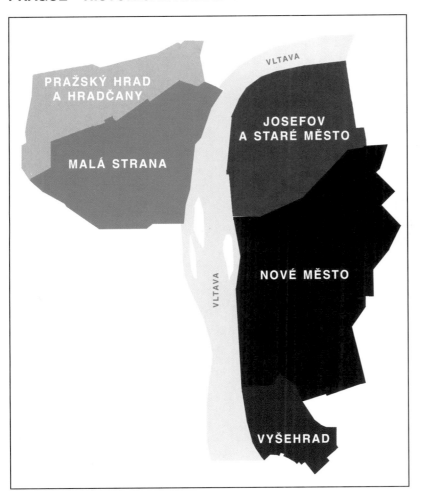

A view of Charles Bridge from Kampa (around 1840), water colour.

The oldest pictures of Prague to have been preserved date from 1493 (drawn by Michael Wohlgemut and Wilhelm Pleydenwurf).

Seven Prague Superlatives, Seven Places in Prague you should certainly see

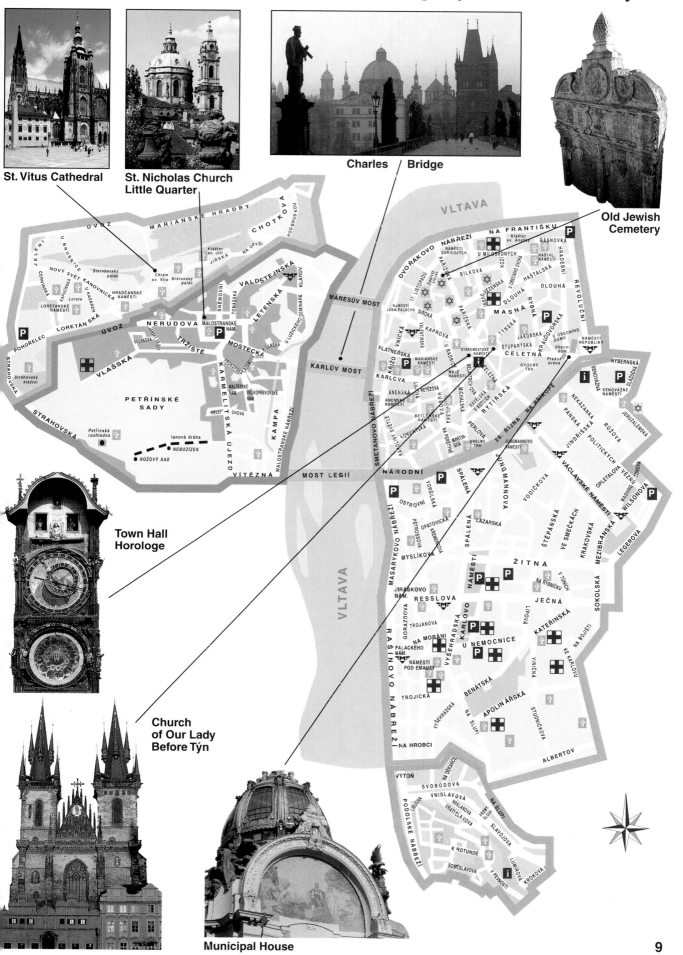

St. Vitus Cathedral

St. Nicholas Church Little Quarter

Charles / Bridge

Old Jewish Cemetery

Town Hall Horologe

Church of Our Lady Before Týn

Municipal House

Seven Prague Superlatives, Seven Places in Prague you should certainly see

The Cathedral of St. Vitus in Prague Castle is the spiritual centre of our state and an architectural gem. It was built in 1344, when the Prague bishopric was promoted to an archbishopric, by King John of Luxemburg and his sons, Charles (later the Bohemian King Charles IV.) and Jan Jindřich. It was not the first church on that site, being preceded by the original Romanesque rotunda, which was later rebuilt as a basilica. The idea of the Luxemburgs - especially Charles - to build a Gothic cathedral there, was speedily carried out. Matthias of Arras, the first builder, constructed eight chapels in the east end of the cathedral between 1344 and 1352. The next builder during Charles's reign was Petr Parléř, who arched the nave with reticulated vaulting, used for the first time in central Europe in this church. Portraits of these two builders and those who followed them, also members of royal families and Prague archbishops, are to be found in the gallery of stone busts - a unique review of sculptural art - in the triforium of the cathedral.

On the southern side of the cathedral is the Golden Gate, once the main entrance. There is a precious mosaic on its facade, dating from 1370-1371 and made from a design by Italian masters of split quartze and glass, representing the Last Judgment. The Gothic support system of the cathedral is surprising - it imitates a town, with turrets, gables, steps and railings. The exterior was indeed intended to portray a town - a divine city. The gargoyles are worth noticing. These incredible monsters, devils and other evil beings, are not the builder's idle fantasies - they are there to protect the cathedral from attack by unclean forces, for superstition says that if a demon sees his own picture on the face of a building, he takes fright and flies away.

The western facade of the cathedral - through which you will enter - is neo-Gothic, and between the two tall towers there is a splendid rose window. Before going in it is worth while noticing the bronze entrance gate, which illustrates the history of the building of the cathedral.

The cathedral's interior lives up to expectations evoked by its exterior. Points of interest are the side chapels with their stained glass windows, works of art both of painting and sculpture, the graves of the Bohemian kings and the tomb of St. John of Nepomuk, above all the St. Wenceslas chapel. This last is the most precious place in the cathedral, containing the relics of St. Wenceslas, the patron saint of the Czech Lands. The chapel was built in 1344-1364 by Petr Parléř and its decoration is an example of the high standard of Czech 14th century art.

The church of St. Nicholas

This church is the dominant building of the Little Quarter and is the best example of Prague high baroque. It was built in 1704-1756 by Kryštof Dientzenhofer, his son Kilián Ignác Dientzenhofer and Anselm Lurago (the belfry). The two towers - the belfry and the dome with a turret - are 79 metres high. The belfry of the St. Nicholas church, which seems to be a permanent part of it, actually never belonged to the church. The stone city emblem over the entrance to the tower is a reminder that it has always been the property of the town.

The dramatic baroque style is mainly in evidence in the interior of the church, where the wealth of form is amplified by contrasts of light. The ceiling fresco over the nave shows the Glorification of St. Nicholas, it dates from 1761 and measures some 1,500 square metres, which makes it one of the largest in Europe. The fresco in the dome - the Glorification of the Holy Trinity - dates from 1751. Beneath the dome are four large statues of the Doctors of the Church by Ignác Platzer (from 1769). The copper statue of St. Nicholas on the main altar is by the same sculptor. The side chapels are decorated with ceiling paintings of those saints to whom the chapels are dedicated. There is a beautiful organ in the church from the mid-17th century, on which Mozart is said to have played.

The Charles Bridge

This jewel of medieval architecture has a secret significance in its beginning. The day the foundation stone of the bridge was laid by the Emperor Charles IV. himself - 9th July 1357 at half past five and one minute - was decided by astrologers, for at that time there was a conjunction of the sun and Saturn, which according to medieval beliefs was the best and most favourable moment of the whole year. The

bridge, as well as the Old Town Bridge Tower, was built by Petr Parléř. It began to be used in 1383, but building on it continued till the beginning of the 15th century. The bridge rests on 16 arches and is 520 metres long, making it one of the longest medieval bridges in Europe. As it has towers at both ends, it was not only a link between the river banks but an important strategic point. The Old Town Bridge Tower is remarkable for its sculptural decoration. The eastern facade of the tower is a glorification of Emperor Charles IV., who founded it. There are statues of the rulers - Charles IV. and his son Wenceslas IV. - with the patron saint of the bridge St. Vitus, and also of the Czech patron saints, as well as quite realistic scenes from everyday life. At the Little Quarter end of the bridge there are two towers. The lower one, built before 1135, was originally Romanesque and was part of the fortifications of the Judith Bridge, which preceded the Charles Bridge. It was later rebuilt in Renaissance style. The taller tower was built in 1464, and was intended as more or less a twin to the Old Town Bridge Tower at the other end.

At first the bridge was decorated only with a simple cross, the statues originating from the 17th century. There are 30 of them altogether, most of them dating from the end of the 17th and beginning of the 18th centuries. They form a beautiful open air gallery. One of the oldest is the Calvary (only the Crucifix), the bronze statue of Christ having been cast in 1629. One of the most effective is the group statue "St. Luitgarde's Dream" by Matyáš Bernard Braun, dating from 1710, one of the best known is the group of St. John of Matha, St. Felix of Valois and St. Ivan, known in Prague as "The Prague Turk" by F. M. Brokof, and one of the most frequently visited is the statue of St. John of Nepomuk. This dates from 1683 and the relief on its pedestal is worn quite smooth, which shows how many wishes the saint has heard from visitors to Prague. Surely they will be fulfilled.

The Old Town Horologe

is located in the tower of the Town Hall, which was completed in 1364. The tower is 69.5 metres high, it has four floors with a gallery and corner turrets, and has always been a symbol of the status of the city. In 1410 an astronomical clock, or horologe, was put up on it by the royal clock-maker, Mikuláš of Kadaň and the astronomer, Jan Šindel, a master of Prague university. About 1490 this unusual work was adjusted and supplemented by Master Hanuš of Růže. It was said to have been unparalleled in Europe. Probably about 1659 the polychrome wooden figures were added. The allegorical statues of Avarice, Vanity and Passion represent the vices, the archangel Michael, with his shield and flaming sword from the Last Judgment, represents one of the basic virtues - Justice.

The horologe consists of three parts, one above the other: the march of the apostles, the astronomical clock-face and the calendarium.

Every hour the apostles file past, followed by Christ blessing the crowds, every hour the skeleton rings a bell to show that yet another hour has passed of the human pilgrimage on earth.

The astronomical clock-face shows the world according to the old geocentric ideas, with the centre marking the geographical position of Prague. The surface represents the universe - daytime, dawn, twilight and night. Circling the sphere are three gold rings - the Tropics of Cancer and Capricorn and the equator.

The calendarium is formed of a circular copper disc divided into two annuli. The inner one contains twenty-four medallions by Josef Mánes from 1866

(copies). The smaller medallions portray the signs of the zodiac, the bigger ones scenes from village life throughout the year.

It is a remarkable fact that the Old Town clock, even after many repairs, still works on the same system on which it was constructed.

The church of Our Lady Before Týn

is the dominant building not only of the Old Town Square, but of the whole of Prague's historic core. It began to be built in the middle of the 14th century on the site of a former little church (early Gothic and Romanesque). Petr Parléř's works took over the construction of the new church from 1380. The towers are 80 metres high and each has 4 turrets. Between the towers is a great late Gothic gable (from 1463), which used to bear a statue of the Hussite King George of Poděbrady and a Hussite chalice. For the Týn church was one of those that belonged to the Reformation tradition, and the reformers Tomáš Műnzer, Konrád Waldhauser and Jan Milíč of Kroměříž

preached there. After the Battle of the White Mountain and the suppression of the Reformation in Bohemia the statue of the "Hussite king" was torn down in 1623 and replaced by a statue of the Virgin Mary. The Hussite chalice was made into her halo.

The northern portal of the church, built by Petr Parléř's works, is a masterly work of art, and one of the most valuable memorials of the high Gothic period. The relief over the doors represents Christ's suffering and crucifixion. The tiny figures in the relief are the spirits leaving the bodies of the dying thieves: devils are fighting for one of them, while the other is being taken to heaven by angels.

The entrance to the church is through a passage in the building of the Týn school. The interior contains numerous works of art from the baroque and Renaissance periods as well as the period when the church itself was built, that is Gothic.

The Old Jewish Cemetery

is one of the most extraordinary places in Prague. It is one of the best kept and oldest Jewish cemeteries in the world. It was founded at the beginning of the 15th century almost in the middle of the Jewish Town. Its restricted area was not enough for the needs of the community and, as religious custom forbids Jews to disturb old graves, more and more layers of earth had to be spread over the existing surface, so that the dead could be buried in them. So that in some places there are as many as twelve burial layers piled upon one another. The old

gravestones were not covered, but always raised to the surface, which is the reason for the peculiar assembly of tombstones. There are almost 12,000 tombstones in the cemetery, dating from 1439 to 1787, when burial of the dead was forbidden in the town. Many of the stones are decorated with various signs and symbols, which express the origin, name or profession of the deceased. One of the most visited places in the cemetery is the tomb of Jehuda ben Becalel, known as Rabbi Low. His name is wreathed in legend and myth, the best known being the story of his creation of an artificial man - a golem.

The Municipal House of the Capital City of Prague

is one of the most important Art Nouveau buildings in Prague. The Municipal House was projected as a centre of spiritual and social life and a symbol of the capital city of the Czech state. The Art Nouveau building was erected from plans by architects Antonín Balšánek and Osvald Polívka in 1905-1911, on the site where the Royal Court once was - the temporary residence of the Bohemian kings, as can be seen from a memorial tablet on the corner of the building. In view of the significance of the Municipal House, leading Czech painters and sculptors were invited to decorate both the exterior and the interior. The facade is topped by a dome with a mosaic by Karel Špillar,

"Homage to Prague". The statues at the sides by Ladislav Šaloun represent the Humiliation and the Resurrection of the Nation. The sides of the building are also richly decorated.

The Smetana Hall is the central hall of the house, the scene of concerts and various social events. At the sides of the podium there are allegorical groups "Czech Dances" and "My Country" by Ladislav Šaloun, and the murals in the balconies personifying Music, the Dance, Poetry and Drama are the work of Karel Špillar. The Municipal House contains a number of halls and clubrooms of a high artistic standard, galleries, a casino, restaurants and cafés. One of the most beautiful rooms is the Lord Mayor's salon - opposite the Smetana Hall - which is decorated with allegorical paintings by Alfons Mucha.

The Prague Castle

(Map of Prague Castle with labeled locations)

Labels on map: MARIÁNSKÉ HRADBY, CHOTKOVY SADY, KRÁLOVSKÁ ZAHRADA, JELENÍ PŘÍKOP, U PRAŠNÉHO MOSTU, ZLATÁ ULIČKA, STARÉ ZÁMECKÉ SCHODY, LEDEBURSKÁ ZAHRADA, VALDŠTEJNSKÁ, VIKÁŘSKÁ, JIŘSKÁ, VALDŠTEJNSKÉ NÁMĚSTÍ, MALOSTRANSKÁ, JIŽNÍ ZAHRADY PRAŽSKÉHO HRADU, SNĚMOVNÍ, TOMÁŠSKÁ, VALDŠTEJNSKÁ ZAHRADA, LETENSKÁ, ZÁMECKÉ SCHODY

1. Matthias Gateway
2. Chapel of the Holy Rood
3. St. Vitus Cathedral
4. Window by Alfons Mucha
5. Royal oratory
6. Tomb of St. John of Nepomuk
7. Tombs of the Přemyslide princes
8. Royal Mausoleum
9. Sculpture Gallery in the triforium
10. St. Wenceslas Chapel
11. Golden Gate
12. Statue of St. George
13. Old Diet
14. Vladislav Hall
15. Church of All Saints
16. Basilica of St. George
17. Golden Lane
18. Prague Castle's Southern Gardens
19. Royal Garden
20. Singing Fountain
21. Royal Summer Palace

Prague Castle

St. Vitus Cathedral

(Floor plan of St. Vitus Cathedral with numbered locations)

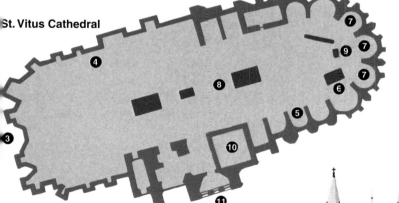

Vladislav Hall

Royal Summer Palace

Charles IV.

Basilica of St. George

Matthias Gateway

The Prague Castle was founded between 880 - 890 by the tribe of the Přemyslides. This pre-Romanesque fort - very extensive for its time - was protected by earthworks and a wooden palisade. By the end of the 9th century this compact fort became the centre of the growing Přemyslide state.

The temporal power strongly supported the rise of the new religion - Christianity - and so increased the role of the church, which led in 973 to the foundation of the Prague bishopric. The seat of the bishop was in the Castle, thus confirming that this place was not only the secular centre of the state, but also the spiritual one.

In the 10th century the main scenes of events in the area of Prague Castle were the princely palace and the churches that were in building.

The oldest church, founded by Prince Bořivoj I. and dedicated to the Virgin Mary, stood on the site of an old heathen place of sacrifice in the western part of the Castle (now the first courtyard) and was probably built of wood. The first all-stone building was the rotunda of St. Vitus, founded after 926 by Prince Wenceslas. This rotunda was the main episcopal church until 1061. The buildings of the princely palace also had stone foundations.

The second oldest church in the area of Prague Castle is the church of St. George, founded around 920 by Prince Vratislav. Soon afterwards the first Benedictine convent was founded next to this church (after 973) by Mlada, the sister of Boleslav II. The daughters of the Bohemian ruling house were educated in this convent. The original little church (founded by Prince Vratislav) was rebuilt as a basilica with a nave and two aisles, the oldest in Bohemia.

But to return to the predecessor of Prague Castle's dominant - the cathedral of St. Vitus. The remains of the rotunda of St. Vitus are still visible beneath the church. Archeological research has shown that the rotunda was a masterly work for its time, and the Czech chronicler Cosmas reports that it was a place of pilgrimage, especially on St. Wenceslas's Day. This fact induced Prince Spytihněv II. (ruled 1055-1061) to build a new, big basilica dedicated to St. Vitus, Wenceslas and Adalbert. This extensive and spacious building was for long the dominant of the Castle.

But past times were turbulent. Strife among the ruling princes, battles with expansive neighbours, plundering and fires destroyed what had previously been built with so much effort.

After every fire or assault the Castle underwent rebuilding, but this was always to its benefit and added to its dignity. Here especially the efforts of Přemysl Ottakar II. (ruled 1253-1278) should be mentioned, as his building activity aimed mainly at strengthening the fortifications and adapting the Royal Palace to make it more imposing and more comfortable to live in. After Přemysl Ottakar's death little building was done at the Castle, and the Přemyslide Royal Palace was destroyed by fire soon after its reconstruction.

Good days dawned for Prague Castle with the coming of Charles IV. to Bohemia (ruled 1346-1378). This monarch and his builders brought a new style to Prague - Gothic. Charles was greatly interested in the seat of his ancestors, so he immediately started rebuilding the Castle. By extending the old core of the building a large and splendid two-storied, French-style palace grew up, with two halls and an oriel chapel of Our Lady. Then Charles IV. turned his attention to building an impressive church by rebuilding Spytihněv's basilica. This was partly a political act as, thanks to Charles, the Prague bishopric had just been promoted to an archbishopric, and this demanded a cathedral worthy of the event. Its building was entrusted to two excellent builders - Matthias of Arras and Petr Parléř. The St. Vitus cathedral is a truly original architectural work, remarkable particularly for its exterior system of flying buttresses.

A later ruler who altered the face of Prague Castle was Vladislav Jagellon (ruled 1471-1516). Like Charles IV. before him, he too made a happy choice of architect. This was Benedikt Ried of Piesting. It was he who built the finest and biggest medieval hall in Prague - the Vladislav hall - which was built for ceremonial gatherings, coronations, banquets, but was also later used for tournaments of chivalry and even markets. Nowadays the most important state events take place there - in the first place the election of the president of the Republic.

The great conflagration of 1541, that broke out in the Little Quarter, rapidly spread to the Castle and the settlement of Hradčany and damaged many buildings, including the cathedral. The repairs were then made in the new - Renaissance - style. An important architect of that time was Bonifác

Wohlmut, and his best work is the House for Ball Games (in the Royal Castle Garden) put up for the ball games fashionable amongst the aristocrats. Under Emperor Rudolph II. (ruled 1576-1611) too there was much building activity at the Castle. The Castle had become an important centre of the empire and of the sciences and art. A new northern palace was built with two great halls - the gallery of Rudolph II. and the Spanish hall, intended for court festivities. Although the Spanish hall was later restored in neo-Baroque style, it remained one of the most beautiful halls of the Castle.

Towards the end of Rudolph's reign, but more during that of his successor Emperor Matthias (1611-1619), a new style - Baroque - entered Prague, and the first secular Baroque building in Bohemia was Matthias's Gateway to the Castle. But the Baroque period was not only creative, it was also a period of destruction. The wars over the Habsburg heritage damaged the Castle badly.

When Maria Theresa ascended the throne extensive re-building of the Castle took place once again. The Italian architect Nicolo Paccassi gave the panorama of Hradčany a new classicist form. It was also his idea to fill in the old moat that had so far separated the Castle from Hradčany and the first courtyard, the court d'honneur, was formed, closed by the gateway with Platzer's statues. So the Castle and Hradčany were optically linked.

The ruler's seat was approaching its definitive form, but the same was not true of the St. Vitus cathedral. There were further plans to complete it in the eighteen-thirties. Canon Václav Pešina founded the Union for the Completion of St. Vitus Cathedral to collect money for this purpose. Work was started according to plans by J. Mocker and continued under his successor Kamil Hilbert. The completion was planned for the thousandth anniversary of the death of Prince Wenceslas (1929). But in 1925 the old and new parts of the cathedral were already joined into a single whole.

Prague Castle is a unique architectural compound of world significance. It is a treasure-house of building styles from Romanesque times until the present day. It is a treasure-house of precious works of art and cultural memorials.

The statues of the Giants over the Gateway to Prague Castle
The figures of the fighting giants were made by the sculptor Ignác Platzer the elder in 1768.

The Matthias Gateway to Prague Castle
is the entrance to the grounds of Prague Castle. It was built during the reign of Emperor Matthias in 1614 by the architect G. M. Filippi and is the oldest baroque building in Prague.

In the middle of the second Castle courtyard there is an early baroque fountain - the work of stonemason Francesca de Torre, with statues by the sculptor J. Kohl from 1686. In the south-eastern part of this courtyard it is worth noticing the chapel of the Holy Rood, built by A. Luragho in 1758-63. The ceiling paintings in the nave are by V. Kandler.

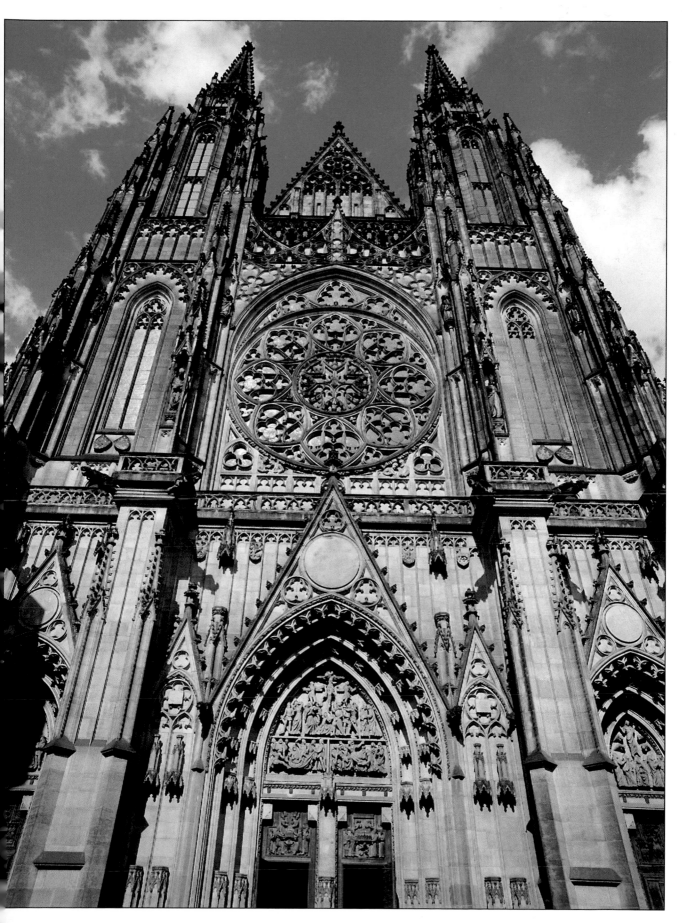

The western facade of the cathedral is neo-Gothic, with two spires 82 metres high (architects Josef Mocker and Kamil Hilbert). The rose window illustrates the various days of the Creation of the World (designed by František Kysela in 1921). The bronze doors of the cathedral portray the history of its building.

Portraits of the main builders of the St. Vitus cathedral, Matthias of Arras and Petr Parléř, which take a place of honour in the sculptural decoration of the triforium.

St. Vitus Cathedral

The original Romanesque rotunda of St. Vitus was founded in the twenties of the 10th century by Prince Wenceslas. It was built at the highest point of Prague Castle and the relics of St. Vitus were preserved in it. Prince Spytihněv had the rotunda torn down and in its place he began to build a basilica, which was completed by his successor, Vratislav II. (1096). When the Prague bishopric was promoted to an archbishopric in 1344 the representatives of ecclesiastical and temporal power decided to build a new church. And so in that year the foundation stone for a Gothic cathedral was laid by John of Luxemburg and his sons, Charles and Jan Jindřich. The first builder in 1344-1352 was Matthias of Arras, who built eight chapels in the east end of the cathedral. After his death the work was taken over by 23-year-old Petr Parléř. During his lifetime he managed to build the remainder of the choir chapels, the triforium and the vault of the choir. He also began to build the transept and the tower.

The cathedral is 124 metres long, 60 metres wide across the transept and the main arch is 33 metres high. The vault over the nave is reticulated and Petr Parléř was the first in Central Europe to use this type of vaulting.